THE BEATLES FOR TWO

Arrangements by Mark Phillips

Cover photo: CBS Photo Archive via Getty Images

ISBN 978-1-5400-4814-1

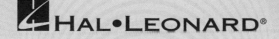

Visit Hal Leonard Online at
www.halleonard.com

Contact us:
Hal Leonard
7777 West Bluemound Road
Milwaukee, WI 53213
Email: info@halleonard.com

In Europe, contact:
Hal Leonard Europe Limited
42 Wigmore Street
Marylebone, London, W1U 2RN
Email: info@halleonardeurope.com

In Australia, contact:
Hal Leonard Australia Pty. Ltd.
4 Lentara Court
Cheltenham, Victoria, 3192 Australia
Email: info@halleonard.com.au

ALL MY LOVING

CLARINETS

Words and Music by JOHN LENNON
and PAUL McCARTNEY

D.S. al Coda

CODA

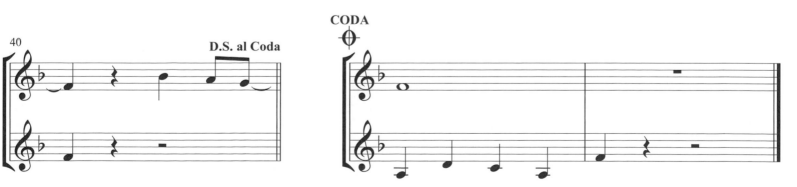

ALL YOU NEED IS LOVE

CLARINETS

Words and Music by JOHN LENNON
and PAUL McCARTNEY

AND I LOVE HER

CLARINETS

Words and Music by JOHN LENNON
and PAUL McCARTNEY

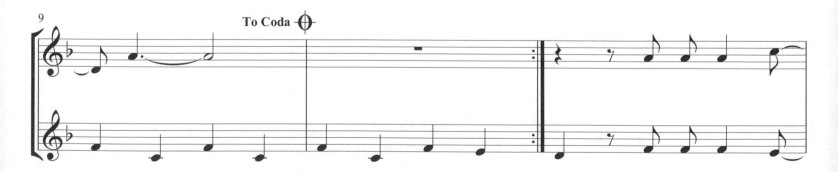

 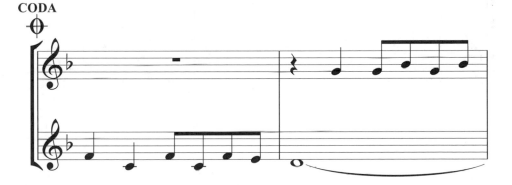

D.S. al Coda
(no repeat)

CODA

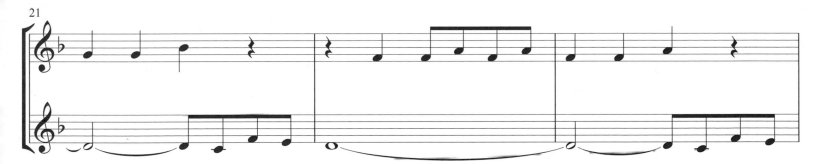

ELEANOR RIGBY

CLARINETS

Words and Music by JOHN LENNON
and PAUL McCARTNEY

Moderately fast

To Coda

D.C. al Coda
(no repeat)

CODA

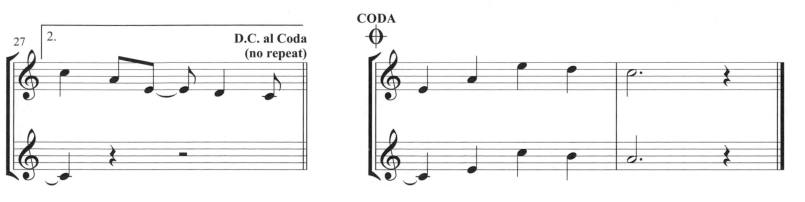

THE FOOL ON THE HILL

Clarinets

Words and Music by JOHN LENNON
and PAUL McCARTNEY

Moderately slow, in 2

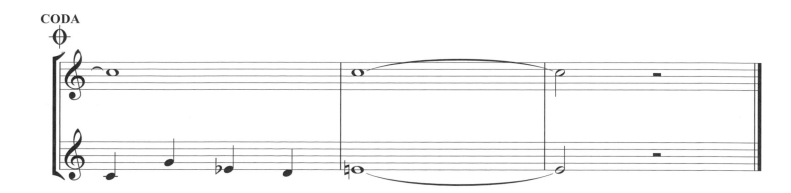

GOLDEN SLUMBERS

Clarinets

Words and Music by JOHN LENNON
and PAUL McCARTNEY

Moderately slow

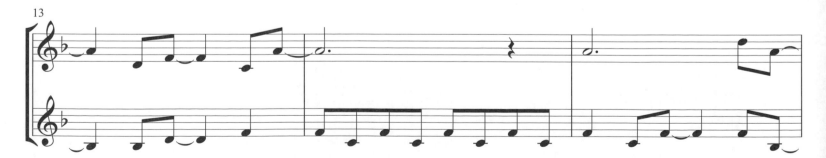

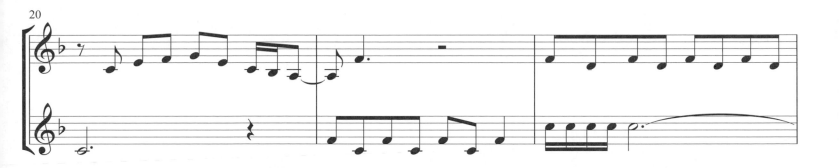

HERE COMES THE SUN

CLARINETS

Words and Music by
GEORGE HARRISON

Moderately fast

HERE, THERE AND EVERYWHERE

Clarinets

Words and Music by JOHN LENNON
and PAUL McCARTNEY

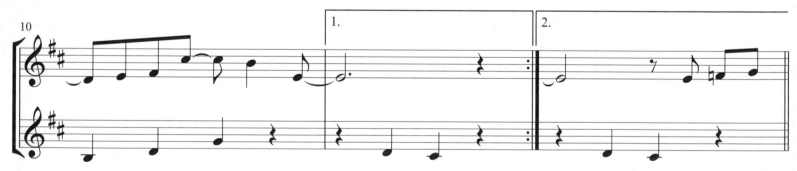

HEY JUDE

CLARINETS

Words and Music by JOHN LENNON
and PAUL McCARTNEY

Moderately

I SAW HER STANDING THERE

CLARINETS

Words and Music by JOHN LENNON
and PAUL McCARTNEY

Moderately fast

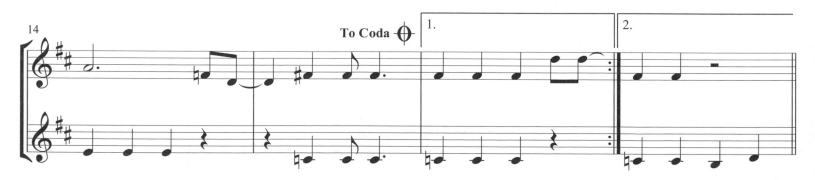

D.S. al Coda
(no repeat)

CODA

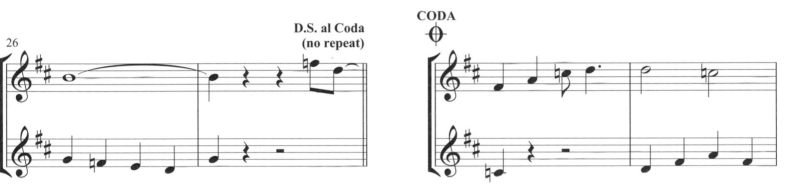

I WANT TO HOLD YOUR HAND

Clarinets

Words and Music by JOHN LENNON
and PAUL McCARTNEY

Moderately fast

CODA

D.S. al Coda
(no repeat)

I WILL

CLARINETS

Words and Music by JOHN LENNON
and PAUL McCARTNEY

Moderately

LET IT BE

CLARINETS

Words and Music by JOHN LENNON
and PAUL McCARTNEY

Moderately slow, in 2

THE LONG AND WINDING ROAD

CLARINETS

Words and Music by JOHN LENNON
and PAUL McCARTNEY

Moderately slow

MICHELLE

CLARINETS

Words and Music by JOHN LENNON
and PAUL McCARTNEY

Moderately slow, in 2

NORWEGIAN WOOD

(This Bird Has Flown)

CLARINETS

Words and Music by JOHN LENNON
and PAUL McCARTNEY

Slowly, in 1

OB-LA-DI, OB-LA-DA

Clarinets

Words and Music by JOHN LENNON
and PAUL McCARTNEY

Brightly, in 2

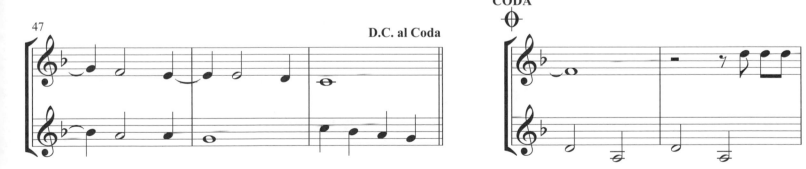

PENNY LANE

CLARINETS

Words and Music by JOHN LENNON
and PAUL McCARTNEY

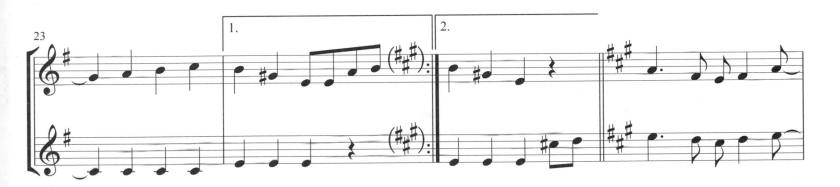

SHE LOVES YOU

CLARINETS

Words and Music by JOHN LENNON
and PAUL McCARTNEY

Moderately fast

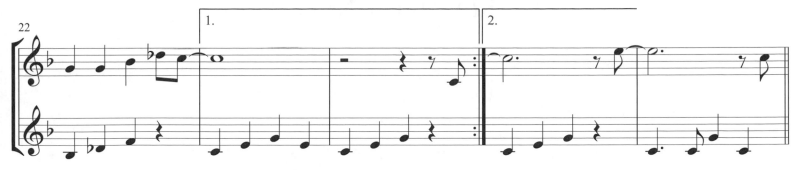

SOMETHING

CLARINETS

Words and Music by
GEORGE HARRISON

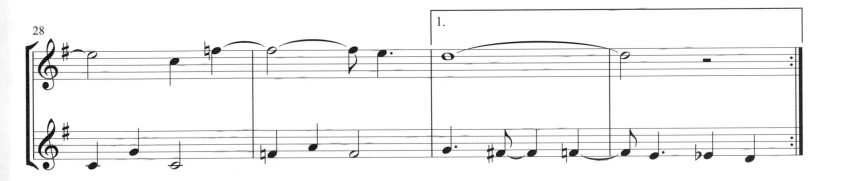

D.S. al Coda
(no repeat)

CODA

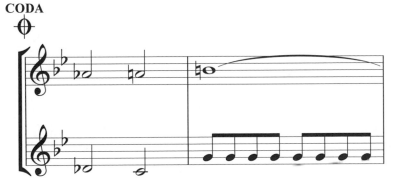

WHEN I'M SIXTY-FOUR

Clarinets

Words and Music by JOHN LENNON
and PAUL McCARTNEY

YELLOW SUBMARINE

CLARINETS

Words and Music by JOHN LENNON
and PAUL McCARTNEY

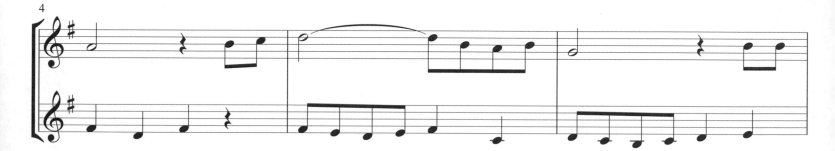

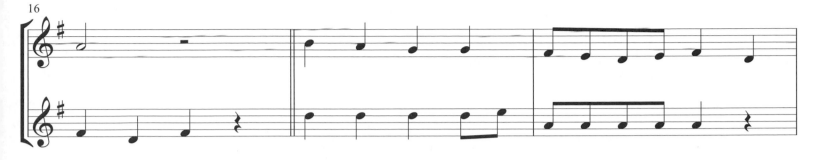

YESTERDAY

CLARINETS

Words and Music by JOHN LENNON
and PAUL McCARTNEY

Moderately

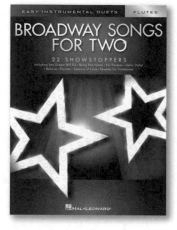